T0062979

OVERCOME YOUR DEPRESSION

A SIMPLE, STEP-BY-STEP,
INTERACTIVE, SELF-HELP WORKBOOK

Jan Hayes

BALBOA
PRESS
A DIVISION OF HAY HOUSE

Balboa Press books may be ordered through booksellers or by contacting:

Balboa Press
A Division of Hay House
1663 Liberty Drive
Bloomington, IN 47403
www.balboapress.com.au
1 (877) 407-4847

Print information available on the last page.

ISBN: 978-1-4525-2800-7 (sc)
ISBN: 978-1-4525-2801-4 (e)

Balboa Press rev. date: 03/25/2015

CONTENTS

INTRODUCTION

Are you fed up with feeling sick and tired?
Have you identified an unwanted condition in your life?

If the miracle had occurred, and the problem had been solved, what could your life be like?

Think about what your life could be like if your depression was cured.
Is this possibility something that motivates you?
Do you want to change?

All humans have the right to be happy and content.

Our aim is to make it happen!

This booklet provides ideas of practical ways to overcome depression and anxiety, presented in a set of simple steps. Included is homework – small but important tasks for you to complete as you work through the strategies.

It will enable you to become more aware of what patterns of thought are reducing your abilities.

The intentions of this book are to help you:

- observe and change inappropriate thoughts, and inspect your 'mind chatter'
- gain assertiveness and interpersonal communication skills through exercises

- understand stress and anxiety, and the negative effects these have on your body
- learn how to improve your self-esteem
- inspect your comfort zones
- understand yourself.

Every action in the universe creates a resonance or vibration. This is true also of emotions. An emotion = energy in motion. An emotion is the body's response to a thought.

Negative emotions such as hatred, anger, resentment, fear and anxiety create negative vibrations at a low frequency. Positive emotions such as love, happiness, enjoyment and fun also emit vibrations. These are of a higher frequency, and are vibrations of a different kind.

Depression is brought about by a chemical change in the body.

Our thoughts, if negative, create our emotions which **create the chemical imbalance,** which in turn creates our depressive state of mind. Our mind is like the hard drive of our body – what is put in will eventually come out. Consider a corrupted computer program; your mind reacts in the same way. What is now required is to extract the unwanted information and input new truths. The mind is primary; what your mind asks for, the body will deliver.

It is impossible to love and connect with others if one lives hidden in misery in an isolated state. All people want to believe they are competent, worthy and loved by others.

We, as humans, were originally programmed to thrive in hunter-gatherer societies, in an intensely social way. 'Clans' looked out for and after each other and their collective children to enable survival. Today, our independent lifestyles – which have an emphasis on independence and mobility – have left us with a quarter of our population living alone. Use of the internet, computers and televisions have all contributed to our separation from others, even inside our own home. Interestingly, our 'social media' has for many created an increasingly anti-social environment, heightening isolation and loneliness.

The importance of social support cannot be overstated. The effect of sharing – the simple process of talking to someone else – is also invaluable. When we talk about our problem, it often alleviates the pressure. So join a group, or talk to friends or family. There are many supportive organisations which have devoted websites and group support for people with depression. Knowing others are going through the same thing helps us to realise we are not isolated in what we feel.

However, before a real and lasting recovery is possible you must inspect your illogical thoughts and beliefs. Illogical means lacking sense or reasoning. These intrusive, distorted and dysfunctional thoughts are the cause of your depression, and can lead to severe anxiety and burnout. When our mind is bombarded with negatively produced hormones and other chemicals, the inevitable happens… a change in our body chemistry. This results in a state of depression.

You must change your negative and inappropriate thinking. Recognising your self-destructive beliefs is the first step toward eliminating them. These destructive beliefs damage your self-esteem, and will prevent you from building meaningful and productive relationships.

Identifying which illogical and false beliefs you currently hold will help you to examine them critically, and will also allow you to see that they are both illogical and self defeating.

This can only be brought about by self-awareness, self-observation, and a willingness to actively change your thinking!

We must continually calm the restless scanning, negative daydreaming, story creation, and largely repetitive and negative chatter and prattle of our rational mind.

What you think leads to what you feel; your emotions.
You are IT... no one else can be held responsible for your emotions.
No one else can be held responsible for your depression.

If you like the rut you are in then read no more.
Apathy and inertia will keep you in a state of suffering.
Alternatively, if you want to enjoy your life you need read on to...

Change your mind and take charge of your thinking!
Now is your chance to do something!

Frequently an event or situation triggers the current depressive state, such as a bereavement, relationship break-up, family conflict, elevated and continual stress, or a major life change. There may be an earlier event in your life which has resurrected, or continues to haunt you.

However, it is not essential to understand what started your depressive state to begin your recovery and improve your ability to overcome it.

This course employs constructive ways to help sufferers identify and overcome problem emotions, and develop coping skills and techniques to help them enjoy good mental health and a happier life.

Now, having said that, if you are taking medication... please continue. See your doctor before changing or stopping any of your meds.

If you follow this course and complete the exercises,
you will never be the same again. You will experience
a noticeable improvement in the way you feel.
There is no going back... only forward!

Ask yourself now:

What do I want to do with my life?
What is stopping me from doing it?
What am I going to do about it?

MY CONTRACT FOR CHANGE (please fill it in)

I,.., take personal responsibility for creating change in my life.

I will begin this course to overcome my depression, and formally make a contract with myself to see this workbook through. I want my life to change, and today is the start of my new life.

Signed.....................................dated......................................
(When we make a written contract to make a change, it helps us stick to our resolve)

DEPRESSION – WHAT ARE SOME OF THE SIGNS?

Feelings of overwhelming sadness
Crying spells
Mood changes – anger, rage
Pessimism and negative self-talk
Lack of satisfaction
Feelings of loneliness or despair
A sense of failure or of worthlessness
Guilty feelings
A sense of punishment
Self dislike
Self accusation
Suicidal thoughts
Irritability
Social withdrawal – feeling that you don't want to go out
Indecisiveness
Distorted body image
Work inhibition, inability to get going
Tiredness
Loss of appetite or increased appetite
Weight loss
Sleep preoccupation or an inability to sleep
Loss of sex drive
Loss of motivation
Slowness in movement
Change in ability to tolerate pain or being more sensitive
Change in capacity to experience pleasure
Noise sensitivity
Alcohol abuse
Panic attacks

If you experience a number of the above symptoms, remember you are not alone. If you haven't sought medical help, then do so now. Anti-depressants can help us to feel better. However, they may not cure the problem... that's up to you.

This is because **only by changing ourselves, can we actually affect a cure.**

Recovery begins when you consciously decide you've had enough, and you want to stop doing whatever it is that's causing your self destruction.

Keep reading... all will be revealed!

MOOD QUESTIONNAIRE

Below is a mood/feeling exercise. Please fill it in before you begin. You will complete another at the end of the course.

Circle the number which indicates how you are feeling right now. Under 5 is a negative mood (1 the lowest), above 5 is positive (10 the highest).

Keeping score of how you feel out of ten

Name

Date

Mood

I feel sad and gloomy   1 2 3 4 5 6 7 8 9 10   I'm the happiest I've ever felt

Confidence

I feel like hiding in a corner   1 2 3 4 5 6 7 8 9 10   I could stand up and give a public speech

Self esteem

I feel worthless   1 2 3 4 5 6 7 8 9 10   I'm on top of the world

How much I feel
like changing

I can't be 1 2 3 4 5 6 7 8 9 10 I want a big life
bothered to do makeover
anything

Hope for the future

I can't believe 1 2 3 4 5 6 7 8 9 10 I'm very hopeful
anything will get life will be better
better

Add up the numbers and record your score.......................

But, **do not judge.** As you are recording what you are feeling right now, this exercise is just a simple way to keep note of your progress and improvement. It shouldn't involve any judgement.

If you're reading this book then your mood may be in the lower areas. At the end of this course one would hope and expect that your score will improve.

The journey of a thousand miles
begins with only one step

Lao Tzu

HANDLING MIND CHATTER

The mind is the master controller of your body – the primary source of your thoughts and actions. What you think becomes your reality. What you concentrate on, you will bring about.

The first step toward recovery is simply to notice what the mind is saying. For some of us, this is the hardest part, because many of us do not notice what we think.

To enable you to get well you must now begin to take control of your mind and thoughts.

What is a negative emotion? A negative emotion is one that is toxic to the body and interferes with its balance and harmonious functioning. Negative emotions include fear, anxiety, anger, intense dislike, hatred, jealousy, sadness, resentment and envy. All these disrupt energy flow in the body, affecting the immune system, digestion, and the production of hormones, thereby contributing to physical and mental disease.

Alternatively, joy, love and peace are states of being which come from within your true nature, and strengthen your immune system, invigorating and healing the body.

Up until now it's possible that the voice inside your head has been telling sad, anxious or angry stories about yourself and your life, about other people, and about the past, future or imaginary events. The voice may be blaming, accusing, complaining or imagining. Perhaps you have been believing the distorted things your inner voice says. At this point the unhappiness has set in and a vicious circle ensues.

You can now learn to break the habit of accumulating and perpetuating of old emotions. You must learn to continually return to the present moment, rather than be obsessed with your mental 'stories'. If you don't, your mind will go on and on spinning its tales, continually reviving old emotion.

Humans limit themselves through grievances, hostility, regret, guilt and shame. It is time to learn how to squash the self sabotage. Using logic and rational responses you can begin to change these unwanted thought patterns.

Let's make a start. We will begin by just noticing what your mind is saying, that is, the types of thoughts that go through your mind. There must be no judgment about this, just observe what you notice about your thoughts.

DISTORTED THINKING STYLES (COGNITIVE DISTORTIONS)

Psychiatrist A.T. Beck and Dr. David Burns' in-depth research has identified a number of common cognitive distortions. See references below for further recommended reading on this subject.

Cognitive distortions or inappropriate, distorted thoughts are prevalent and negative ways that our mind has developed to convince us of something about us that is not true. These inaccurate core beliefs, or illogical thoughts about ourselves, act to reinforce negative thinking and create distressing and unwanted emotional responses.

We continually tell ourselves things that sound rational and accurate, but often they are untrue, and really only serve to keep us feeling bad about ourselves and others. They perpetuate emotional disturbance and sickness.

Remember that your emotions follow your thoughts, and negative emotions are not actually reflective of the real or true situation. They reflect only what you have just thought.

Below are some common cognitive distortions, also called 'inappropriate thought patterns'. 'Inappropriate' may even be too bland a description, because some of these thoughts become toxic. That is, they become dangerous, destructive and harmful to our health. They keep us feeling bad and sad.

- **All-Or-Nothing thinking**

You see things in black and white categories. The thought is that the event is either perfect or totally useless. This reinforces negative feelings. There is no middle ground.

- **Overgeneralisation**

The word 'always' often accompanies overgeneralisation. For example, *"I always fail"*, *"I'm always a loser"* or *"Everyone thinks I'm stupid"*. In this thought pattern, you think one single negative event is a continual pattern. If you make a slight error you conclude you're stupid, and this is what you say to yourself.

- **Mental Filter**

You pick out a single negative detail and focus on it exclusively. For example, if your partner doesn't love one of your meals, you tell yourself you're a useless cook and they hate your food.

- **Disqualifying the Positive**

When someone praises your appearance or your work, you might automatically tell yourself *"They're just being nice"* or *"They must be blind"*, thereby rejecting any positive evidence. The price you pay for this way of thinking is intense misery and the inability to appreciate the good things that happen in life.

- **Mind Reading – Jumping to conclusions**

You make a negative interpretation even though there are no definite facts that convincingly support your conclusion.

For example, you automatically conclude that someone is reacting negatively to you. If your partner is particularly quiet you may wrongly conclude, *"He is ignoring me so he must not like me anymore"*. Or you think your spouse or partner is mad at you because he or she isn't talkative, thinking *"What did I do wrong?"* See how it's all about you? You're not checking out what is really happening. You may then respond to these imagined negative reactions by withdrawal or counterattack. This creates trouble when there was nothing going on in the first place.

- **The Fortune Teller Error**

You predict a bad outcome. Perhaps you have been invited to a party. You convince yourself that no one would be interested in talking to you and so decline the invite.

- **Magnification (Catastrophising or minimisation)**

You envisage worst case scenarios. This occurs when you turn your own errors, fears or imperfections into larger problems, exaggerating their importance. If you make a mistake you conclude *"This is a total disaster".* You also discount your own good qualities or other people's failings.

- **Emotional Reasoning**

You assume that the way you feel reflects the way things really are. In other words, because things feel so negative to you, you assume they truly are. (Remember, your thoughts create your emotions, so you cannot rely on your feelings when you are depressed.) It doesn't occur to you to challenge the reason that you feel bad. That is, you don't question or dispute the things you are saying to yourself.

In essence, just because you feel it's true, doesn't mean it is. You cannot trust your feelings right now! These thought patterns are typical of a depressed state of mind.

- **Should Statements**

In this inappropriate thought pattern, you believe you have to live up to ridiculously high standards, and you may also reflect these onto others. For example, you may say *"You should do it this way"* or *'I'm stupid, I should have done it that way",* making yourself and others wrong.

The emotional consequence is guilt. When you direct 'should' statements toward others, you feel anger, frustration and resentment. When you direct them to yourself, you will also feel guilty and frustrated.

- **Labelling and Mislabelling**

For instance when you make a mistake, you may think *"I'm a born loser"* instead of *"I just made an error, no sweat"*. Labelling yourself is not only self defeating, it is also irrational and untrue. Your life is an ever-changing flow of thoughts, emotions, moods and actions. Stop trying to define yourself with negative labels – THEY ARE WRONG.

Labelling others (name calling) will invariably generate hostility too, plus these are judgments, which we shall discuss later.

- **Personalisation**

You see yourself as the cause or assume responsibility for events that really had nothing to do with you. For example *"It's all my fault"* or *"Everything I do is wrong"*. You are left feeling guilty for no genuine reason.

Your feelings are not facts. If your distorted thoughts make no sense, the feelings they create will be also false.

So, the key to releasing yourself from your emotional prison is simply this:
Your thoughts create your emotions, therefore your emotions cannot prove that your thoughts are accurate. **In fact, they are most assuredly WRONG.** Unpleasant feelings merely indicate that you are thinking something negative and believing it.

Your emotions follow your thoughts. Yes, **your emotions follow your thoughts.**

So the answer is: take control of your thoughts.

You can quite easily make yourself upset by reliving in your head a particularly sad or gloomy experience. Go on, try it now... see how thinking about something negative makes you FEEL BAD. You can even make yourself cry just by thinking about a sad event. Similarly, if you imagine a happy event or a joke you may smile or giggle. The body responds to a thought.

When you shift wrong assumptions you will experience an enhanced emotional life with a greater appreciation for genuine sadness as well as joy.

You must modify the illogical thinking patterns, shattering the wrong ideas you hold about yourself and others, and increase your capacity for a happier life. The only way to achieve this is to monitor what you are thinking.

Moment by moment ask yourself "What thoughts are going through my mind right now? What am I saying to myself? Why is this upsetting me? How can I respond to that thought?" This process will allow you to see the errors in your thinking.

At the beginning, this thought and emotional observation is not easy, but with practice becomes so.
After you start to get the hang of recognising the thoughts that are causing the negative feelings, the next step is to challenge them.

Once you have observed the inappropriate thoughts, you can then learn to install new and positive voices in your head. Through continually pinpointing distortions in your automatic thoughts, you can break a bad habit.

Let's look at how you can modify your negative ways of thinking. I suggest you keep a journal of what you are thinking and feeling. This way, you can see what distorted patterns of thought are stopping your progress.

Jan Hayes

Homework

Begin by writing down your own thoughts, then next to that write down the type of distorted thought (from the list of distorted thinking styles on pages 8-10). The next step is to substitute a more rational, sensible and less upsetting thought. Look for the truth.

For instance "*I'm useless*" – this is an **overgeneralisation**, and also a **label**, and actually does not make sense when you challenge it. Your more positive rational response could be "*Actually I am not useless at all, I can do many things well.*"

It is crucial to write down your automatic thoughts, together with their rational, logical and sensible responses. This process forces you to develop more objectivity than you could ever achieve by letting responses swirl through your mind.

Sadness and miserable internal states do not prove that you are a worthless person, but merely that you think you are because you are in a temporarily depressed mood. Depression itself causes us to think these wrongful thoughts.

You are thinking illogically and unreasonably about yourself.

All you have to do is reply to that critical,
nagging internal voice... Why?

Because that critical inner voice is wrong!

Remember three crucial steps when you are upset:

1. Zero in on those automatic negative thoughts and **write them down.** Don't let them buzz around in your head: get them on paper!
2. Read over the list of distorted thoughts. See how you are churning negative ideas and blowing them out of proportion. **Decide which of the distorted thinking styles on pages 8-10 fits your distorted thoughts.**
3. **Respond with a more objective, rational and sensible thought** that challenges the wrongful thinking which made you feel bad about yourself.

For example, when I was depressed, some of my negative automatic thoughts were:

"*Nobody loves me*" which is an **overgeneralisation** and **magnification**, and my rational response was "*Actually, some people do love me*".

"*Everyone criticises me*". Again, an **overgeneralisation** and **magnification**, and my rational response was "*That's not true. Perhaps I was criticised as a child, but that is no longer true.*"

"I must be worthless" – **emotional reasoning** and **labelling**. My rational response was "*That's rubbish. I have many good qualities and have been successful in many things.*"

**Unfortunately, because we feel so bad, these
self-destructive beliefs actually feel true.
But they are not. They are illogical and self-defeating.**

Whenever you become aware of the illogical thought, that's when you must nail it. If you notice it later, don't worry or berate yourself. Just commit to dealing with it next time it arises.

Please use the headings overleaf to identify some of your automatic and flawed thinking.
Write down in your journal what automatically comes into your mind when you self criticise. Then look up the distorted thinking styles on pages 8-10 to see which fits. Lastly, stand up for yourself with a self-defence or sensible response statement which sounds real to you.

Keep following this process, always writing it down, and you will slowly shift those wrong assumptions and begin to feel better.

Please be aware that you are not suppressing your emotions... that would be dangerous and counterproductive. Rather, this exercise is to observe your thoughts and take charge before the emotion arises. Having said that, if you feel emotionally charged, angry even, then it is important to address the problem – perhaps you need to go outside and yell at the sky. Better still, read up on assertiveness and the great 'I' messages later in this booklet.

Further recommended reading on Cognitive Distortions and behaviour
David D. Burns, M.D. "The Feeling Good Handbook" and "Feeling Good: The New Mood Therapy" and also Beck, A.T. (1976). Cognitive therapies and emotional disorders. New York: New American Library.

Let's look at a couple of examples.

1. You have been invited to a party. You automatically decline, but your friend eventually talks you into going.

Automatic thought
(Self-criticism)
"I don't want to go, no one will talk to me, they will all think I'm stupid."

The cognitive distortions in those statements are:
Overgeneralisation *(No one will talk, they will all think.)*
Labelling *(I'm stupid.)*
Mind reading *(They will all think.)*

Your sensible response could be:
"Wait a second, I may enjoy the party. If I talk to someone first I may have a great conversation.
How do I know what people are thinking? I'm being irrational. Let's give it a chance."

2.   You arrive late for class or work.

Automatic thought
"I'm a loser, this is a disaster, I should have left home earlier. Everyone will look at me and think I'm a jerk, and embarrass me."

The cognitive distortions are:
Labelling *(I'm a loser, a jerk.)*
Overgeneralisation *(Everyone will look at me.)*
All-or-Nothing thinking *(This is a disaster.)*
Mind Reading *(They will think I'm a jerk.)*
Magnification *(This is a disaster.)*
Should statements *(I should have left home earlier.)*

Your sensible response could be:
"Don't be silly, this is no disaster and I'm hardly a loser for being late. Perhaps I should have given myself more time, but there is no harm done. I cannot possibly know what people are thinking. Just smile, apologise and get over it!"

What is required now is for you to shatter your self chatter... because it's negative, self sabotaging and perpetuating your depression.

As you do this, you'll begin to feel better. You'll be boosting your self-esteem, and your sense of worthlessness and your depression will diminish.

Remember, the negative 'story' and self judgments are just ideas that you believe to be the truth.

But... **they are not true!**

If the negative or judgemental mind chatter is about another person, ask yourself:

"What do I need to say or do, right now?" (with courtesy, manners and respect)

1. What should I have said or done?
2. What could I have said or done?
3. What didn't I say or do?

Answer... either **do it** or resolve to do it next time. Don't berate yourself, just make sure you change the result on the next occasion. You will then feel good about it, and no thought will be given to the matter once it's handled with integrity. We shall look at the meaning of integrity later in this book.

For example you have been waiting to be served when shopping. The female assistant apparently has not noticed you. You automatically conclude she is ignoring you, and may then tell yourself that she is judging you negatively. You may then begin an internal dialogue like *"Who does she think she is? Someone better than me? I'll give her a piece of my mind!*

The reality is she was distracted and did not see you. All you had to do was say "*Excuse me, may I be served?*"

Thoughts are powerful things, and what we think inevitably become our reality... so take care what you think. Think about only the good things you did, and the good things that happened to you. Do not dwell on the past – it is gone for good, and there's no need to relive it. It is like the wake of a boat, gone past forever, never to be re-visited.

Give up thinking about the past and make peace with the present moment. Ask yourself "Is there negativity in me at this moment?" The moment you become aware of a negative state within yourself, it does not mean you have failed. On the contrary, your new awareness means that you have succeeded!

Now you have to give up complaining, blaming, resentment, and going over old hurts and fears. "*Why do I need to give up criticism, blaming, resentment and complaining?*" you may ask...

Because it's making you sick!

The bottom line is **you must control your thinking**. Watch out for daydreaming – that is, thinking of bad things that happened to us, elaborating on the story, and getting lost in the '*he said, she said, what I should have said or done, what was done to me*' and on and on – because this can also be dangerous. Get control of it... stop it. These types of negative thoughts will contribute to your depression.

At any moment, you can stop this erroneous and even toxic thinking, and choose not to react.

The question is which moment will you choose? Non-reaction is not a weakness, but a strength. Another word for non-reaction is forgiveness.

Never sit in judgment... especially upon yourself.

Whether you believe it or not, when you change your thinking your depression will diminish.

**Give up passing judgment upon yourself and others.
Whatever your story... give it up now.**

"I don't do anything that's bad for me.
I don't like to be made nervous or angry.
Anytime you get upset it tears
down your nervous system."
May West (actress)

Homework check in

Did you do the homework?

So far, you should be writing down your automatic thoughts and identifying the cognitive distortions of self criticism. Do this every day. If you need, check back to the 'Homework' heading on page 12 for the description of how to do this.

Can you see which of the distortions applies to your wrongful thinking? What was your self defence, your rational and sensible response?

CHANGING NEGATIVE VOCABULARY

It's important to alter your vocabulary to reframe your negative statements to more empowering, positive ones. It is now time to upgrade your negative vocabulary to the preferences listed below.

Negative word		Replace with
Must	>	Prefer, will, won't
Should	>	Prefer, would like to, would desire
Have to	>	Choose to
Need	>	Want
Can't	>	Choose not to, prefer not to
Never	>	Rarely
Always	>	Often, frequently
Can't stand it	>	Don't like
Awful	>	Undesirable, wouldn't like it
Bad person	>	Bad behaviour
I'm a failure	>	I was unsuccessful at...

Thoughts and deeds of anger, rage, sadness, criticism, hatred, are all attack thoughts and are making you sick! So... get control of yourself.

When negative thoughts arise, ask yourself... is this an attack thought? If it is then stop it right there.

Just say to yourself, okay, my homework this week is to say no to attack thoughts.

As well as affecting your internal mind frame, reducing your attack thoughts will positively affect your interactions with others. People turn away from those who use negative vocabulary and have negative attitudes.

No attack thoughts or deeds... either toward yourself or toward another.
This works
Start now!

Remember to write in your journal daily. Whenever you are feeling particularly bad, go over the distorted thinking styles and try to identify which ones apply to you.

What can you challenge yourself to confront and refute right now? Buried emotions of rage and resentment are toxic and harmful. They change your physical chemistry and result in your depression.

Some say that depression is anger turned inward. Can you identify buried anger? What are you telling yourself about an event you experienced that caused you to feel anger?

Does a current event trigger an emotion that you have experienced before? Ask yourself "Why do I feel this way? Does this event remind me of an earlier time, an earlier event?".

You may identify an earlier time when you felt this way. If so, it is important to investigate it and understand the feelings the situation generated. Once investigated, you may gain a new insight into the event or situation. If anger is discovered, then express it – get it off your chest. You may want to confront a situation, write a letter, or talk to someone about it. Once it is dealt with, do not revisit it.

When in depression we feel hopeless and worthless. It seems true at the time. Do understand that when your depression lifts, those feelings will also go. If we sometimes feel that the world would be a better place without us, it is the illness telling us this. When we get better we sometimes cannot believe that we actually had suicidal thoughts.

Even if your depression arose from something you had absolutely no control over, now is the time to address the thoughts and emotions that were generated as a result of the event.

Say no to attack thoughts.
Say no to judgments.
Say no to grumbling and
criticising yourself or others.

You may say "But he upset me", or "She hurt my feelings" or "They did this to me".

Please understand that it is your reaction to the event that makes you ill. No one else can make you upset except you. The answer is not 'out there' somewhere... there is no magic wand.

You are it!
You, and only you, can change
the way you feel.
It is your negative thoughts which
cause you to feel depressed.

Do you really want to become hateful and bitter?

Your depression will not leave until you eliminate those attack thoughts.

You will know no peace until you discover how to forgive yourself and others.

Non-reaction is the key. When you stay in a permanent state of non-reaction your body chemistry stabilises and you become healthier and happier. You can allow yourself to feel human, but the bottom line is you have to address the toxic thinking. Writing down your thoughts works best, as it enables you to identify recurring patterns and revise what you were thinking.

COMFORT ZONES

We all have areas we call 'comfort zones'.

Comfort zones include a range of activities where we feel comfortable and at ease. These might include talking to friends, walking, taking a bus, driving a car, going to work or school, using our phone, watching TV. I'm sure you can add a few more.

It's possible that once these were fearful activities, but with persistence and practice we have become adept and relaxed doing them.

When we do something new, we push against the parameters of our comfort zones. If done often enough, we overcome the fear, and our comfort zone expands. If we back off and stay comfortable, our comfort zone shrinks.

If we get stuck or trapped inside our comfort zone, we build a wall of limitation and fear. When we 'give in' to the comfort zone, it contracts. Our world becomes even smaller. Our belief is that we can't do it, we're not worthy, or not good enough, and this prevents us from even thinking about pushing through the comfort zone. We may say we can't be bothered, but this is a cover up. We use rationalisations and excuses, but this only serves to keep us stuck where we are. Nothing changes and nothing happens... we don't do anything. We remain dissatisfied and fearful.

When we expand our comfort zone at every opportunity we become more successful, less fearful and our confidence and self esteem increases. We can become proud of our achievements.

Fear is a part of life. Some people feel fear pushing against their comfort zone. Others feel fear when they think they might get close to the comfort zone. The fear is the same. The expanding person feels the fear only once. The person in the shrinking comfort zone feels the fear often.

Inside the comfort zone we experience:
Fear   Self doubt
Lack of understanding   Lack of growth
Lack of trust in ourselves
Lack of responsibility
Lack of confidence
Uncertainty
Fixed viewpoints

When we get 'stuck' in a comfort zone, we limit our possibilities, happiness and growth. Fear of what's outside stops us.

We must feel the fear and do it anyway! Take a bold step and expand. Do something today that you have been putting off.

Outside the comfort zone we experience:
Fun   Success
Creativity   Growth
Expansion
High activity   Confidence
Possibility   Productivity

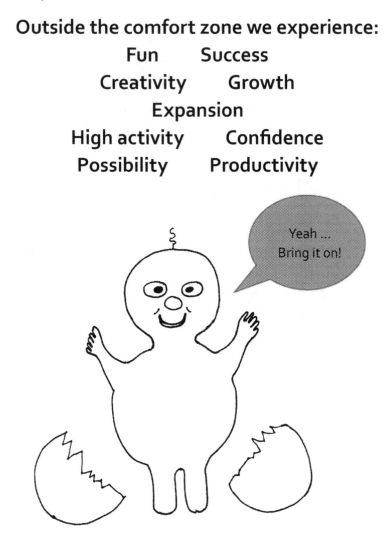

If you want something in your life to
change, you have to do something!

When we expand our comfort zones, we become unlimited,
increasing our self-esteem, confidence and decreasing fear. Life
becomes fun, and we become more successful and creative.

List some of your comfort zones, and **write down what is preventing you from doing something**. What are some of the excuses you use to remain where you are, to stay put in your safe zone?

My comfort zones	What is stopping me?	My excuses

It takes a big effort to get up and do something new.

What can I commit to doing right now?

_____

_____

_____

_____

_____

_____

Remember to make your goals specific, measurable, attainable, realistic and also time limited.

AFFIRMATIONS

An affirmation is a statement of positive fact. They assert a desire to be a certain way, and are worded in the present. Affirmations are positive statements of how you wish to be.

Affirmations possess enormous power they neutralise the negative 'self chatter' continually inside your head. They also increase your well being. Affirmations open up your mind to new 'truths' through eliminating the inappropriate ways of thinking which are not only disempowering you but also keeping you unwell. When saying affirmations, visualise yourself smiling, looking relaxed and happy.

What you concentrate on will become reality. Therefore, when we concentrate on positive affirmations, we have no room for negative dialogue.

Keep a couple of these affirmations on cards in your wallet or in the car, and say them out loud. The more often they're used, the more real, true, solid and firm they become.

Affirmations are very powerful when you repeat them in front of a mirror while looking into your own eyes. All the negative thoughts and feelings that keep you from fulfilling your affirmation will probably surface. Let them surface, and let them float away. Beneath all that 'stuff' is a part of you that knows the truth of the affirmation. You will become what you think about most.

Create your own affirmations to suit your particular situation. Remember to keep them a positive statement of the present. For example, say **"I am healthy, wealthy and happy"**, not "I want to be...' or 'Soon I will be...'.

Here are some examples you may like to try:

- "Every day, in every way, I'm getting better and better."
- "I am worthy of all the good in my life."
- "I forgive myself unconditionally."
- "I love and accept myself and others."
- "I am relaxed and calm, poised and serene."
- "I give myself permission to live, love and laugh."
- "Good things are coming to me now."
- "I am a lovable and worthy person."
- "I deserve to feel good."
- "I am learning to accept and love everyone unconditionally – including myself."

Make up some of your own. Give yourself permission to feel good right now. If you say it like it's already happened, it will happen!

Remember, if you want something, put your attention on it, visualise it, and see it happening right now. You may like to keep an affirmation section in your journal too.

STRESS AND ANXIETY

Our bodies react to a perceived challenge – either mental or physical – by increasing metabolism, elevating blood pressure, boosting heart and breathing rates, and pumping three to four times more blood to the muscles than normal. This creates a 'hyper-alertness'. Activation of this 'fight or flight' defensive system is perfectly normal for brief periods of time. This mechanism works well when we are faced with, say, a possible attack by a tiger... where we must choose to fight or to run.

But in modern times, when this primitive threat response overcomes us, we neither fight nor flee. This is where our physical problems arise.

A surplus of adrenaline and other hormones coursing through our bodies can lead to a host of psychological and physical problems. If you spend a lot of time under serious levels of stress, you may be more at risk for developing depression, even when the stressful events have passed. Interestingly, stress is also 'contagious'. When we are in close contact with another who is stressed out, the stress will also affect us.

Although the body is very intelligent, it cannot tell the difference between an actual situation and a thought. It reacts to every thought as though it were reality. To the body, a worrisome, fearful thought means "I am in danger", and it responds accordingly. The heart beats faster, muscles contract, breathing becomes rapid. There is a build up of energy. But because it has no outlet – since the danger is only a mental fiction – part of it is released back into the mind, and generates even more anxious thought and energy.

This leads to a change in the body's chemistry and harmonious functioning.

When even more stress and anxiety is piled on, the overabundance of flight or fight chemicals becomes toxic, and we become sick.

Factors contributing to anxiety

Artificial stimulants can cause or contribute to anxiety. Caffeine, nicotine, marijuana, amphetamines and cocaine provoke anxiety reactions and personality disturbance. Hallucinations and psychosis can be experienced with some of these chemicals. (Psychosis is a feature of mental illness involving radical changes in personality, impaired functioning, and a distorted or non-existent sense of what is real.) The withdrawal from these chemicals will also cause anxiety.

Alcohol is also problematic, as while some people drink to ease depression, alcohol is a depressive and thus worsens the situation. Drinking more to overcome the depressed state creates a vicious circle. Alcohol is also known to deprive the body of the important B group vitamins.

Many people who experience stress can't stomach big meals, and can often compensate by drinking extra coffee or alcohol, smoking, or eating junk food or skipping meals, thereby stripping the body of the nutrition and energy required to handle stress. This also adds to the stress by interfering with the stable blood-sugar levels needed for energy and well being. In addition, the constant release of adrenaline and other hormones has a negative impact on the heart and immune system.

What you can do to help

Eating small, nutritious snacks throughout the day will improve energy levels. Fruit and vegetables, nuts, wholemeal sandwiches, rice and fish, and occasional lean meat are most beneficial to give the body optimum health and energy. Fish and rice are particularly beneficial as they are rich in B vitamins, the lack of which has been linked with anxiety, irritability, depression and mood swings.

Regular exercise and relaxation are also important. These help alleviate the symptoms of stress.

Symptoms of depression and anxiety

While depression and anxiety disorders have similar symptoms, they are not exactly the same.

Those who suffer from depression may feel hopeless, overwhelmed or angry. Their energy level may be low. They may have problems maintaining relationships.

People who suffer from anxiety disorders experience fear, panic or anxiety in situations where most people don't feel anxious or threatened. Some people experience sudden panic attacks without knowing what the trigger was.

Anxiety is a learned behaviour and becomes a mental disorder when the symptoms are so severe and long lasting that they have a negative effect on a person's life.

It is common for anxiety to accompany depression. However, depression does not always accompany anxiety. Listed below are some debilitating anxiety disorders.

Examples of anxiety disorders

Panic attacks
These occur when the body has heightened responses, even though there is no immediate danger. The 'fight or flight' response sets in. The mind tricks the body into the 'danger alert' mode. You may think you're having a heart attack when it is actually a panic attack, but if this happens still get these symptoms checked out by a doctor.

Obsessive-compulsive disorder
This disorder is characterised by obsessive thoughts that don't go away, and repeating certain behaviours, like washing one's hands or touching certain objects, or mental acts like counting.

Obsessions
Obsessions are all-consuming or compulsive thoughts that won't go away. They can be unwanted, uncontrollable, and often inappropriate.

Compulsions
These develop as a response to obsessions. Sufferers feel compelled to repeat certain physical or mental tasks over and over, helping them find relief from the anxiety of the obsession. The most common obsessions concern thoughts of contamination (i.e. germs). People with this compulsion may fear shaking hands, eating, and opening doors. The most common compulsion is called 'checking', for example repeatedly checking to see if they locked the door, or turned out the lights.

THINGS TO DO
Wash hands
Check window locks
Check door locks

Wash hands
Check window locks
Check door locks
Repeat above

Repeat
Repeat
Repeat

What can help?

If you are suffering from anxiety or depression, it is important that you talk to someone about your feelings. There is no substitute for the opinion and advice of a professional mental health worker or your doctor.

But to help yourself you must **close down the negative self talk**, which stirs it up and can intensify anxiety. Through negative self talk we scare ourselves.

What to do when suffering from anxiety

- When you feel anxious or panicked, breathe calmly and deeply at normal, regular intervals. Avoid rapid short breaths.
- Do your best to stop thinking frightening thoughts.
- However, don't fight your symptoms by trying to wish the feelings away. Willpower is not a solution.

- Don't dwell on how it might get worse. Negativity can result in panic.
- Participate in simple, fun, interesting and safe activities.
- Humour and laughter are good ways to reduce and prevent symptoms of anxiety and panic.
- Avoid drugs – both illegal drugs and any legal drugs that haven't specifically been prescribed to you by your doctor. Avoid alcohol.
- Maintain regular physical activity. This can be an effective way to relieve symptoms and build strength to relieve stress.
- Talk to a mental health professional if you experience recurrent symptoms of anxiety and panic.

The next step is to learn a relaxation technique.

RELAXATION

When you're alone and quiet, negativity decreases while alertness increases. As a result, your ability to think more clearly, be creative and maintain an emotional calm increases. Try to relax for at least 30 minutes each day, even ten minutes is better than not at all.

A relaxation meditation reduces stress, reduces pain, improves the metabolism and lowers blood pressure and enhances brain function. Our immune system is given relief and can repair itself.

Relaxation exercise

Sit comfortably in an upright armchair or sofa. It is best not to lie down or you may fall asleep.

Put on a quiet meditation-type music CD, something soft and pleasant. Turn off your phone and ask the family to please 'shhhh' just for a short while.

Close your eyes and begin by putting your attention on your breathing. Feel it move slowly in and out. With each inward breath imagine peace and calming energy coming into your body. With each exhalation imagine stress, tension and anxiety leaving you.

Now focus on relaxing your body. Start at the toes – wiggle them, then let them go... relax. Move the relaxation up through your ankles, calves and thighs, each time flexing the muscles then letting them relax. Be aware of the weight of your legs. Continue to move the relaxation to your mid-section, muscles firstly tensing, then relaxing. Continue to breathe in and out, focusing on how relaxed you are beginning to feel.

Feel a warm easy feeling flowing up through your body. Keep on breathing in deeply and breathing out gently. Just notice your breath, keep bringing your attention back to your easy breathing.

Continue through your chest, neck, arms, hands and then up to your head. Screw up your face, then let it go. Swallow, then relax the mouth. You may feel comfortably heavy.

You can think *"from the top of my head to the tips of my toes I feel beautifully relaxed, and it feels so good"*. Keep concentrating on your breath, just notice it travelling in and out, very easy. Talk yourself into a pleasant relaxed state.

Your mind will have a tendency to roam. If it does this, just gently bring it back either to your breathing, or to your relaxed state. If you feel an eruption of unpleasant thoughts or feelings, give yourself permission to release them, and allow them to leave through your breath. Observe the thoughts or feelings, then let them go. Insight and release go together. You may see something that is stopping you. Once inspected, ask it to leave you now, and feel relieved afterward.

Tell yourself that it feels good to be so relaxed, and that you feel relaxed and calm, poised and serene.

At this time you can begin with your **affirmations**. Just say them in your head and while saying them see yourself happy, smiling and calm. You may like *"Good things are coming to me now"* or *"Every day in every way I'm getting better and better"*.

True meditation is actually the still space where nothing is going on and you are just a quiet, breathing being. In this state, there are no thoughts, just utter tranquillity. This advanced meditation takes a little more practice, but any practice in which you relax and focus on your breathing is beneficial, even if thoughts pass through your mind. Be mindful not to criticise yourself when thoughts appear.

When meditating you may experience pleasant sensations such as tingling, buzzing, serenity, feeling weightless. You may have insights. Your breathing gets slower. Don't worry about any of these, your body knows what to do.

These techniques **do work.** Try it. Have you heard of the phrase 'fake it till you make it'? That's just the way it works. Your mind and body react to your internal dialogue. Make it a good one!

*Just breathing in... and out... in... and
out... in... and out....relaxed and calm*

**Say no to attack thoughts or attack actions
.... Say no to judgments,
especially toward yourself**

SELF-ESTEEM

Self-esteem means to 'appreciate the worth of self'. It is how we view and think about ourselves and the value that we place on ourselves. It is the most important and basic quality of a healthy, happy human being. It is the basis of our ability to live with integrity, to be trusting and trustworthy, to love others and to attempt challenges without debilitating fear.

Self-esteem must be nurtured and built up. Like a muscle, if it is not worked and strengthened, it will atrophy. This is what happens when we suffer with depression. People suffering from depression frequently have a low self-esteem.

What do I think of myself?
How do you describe yourself?

_____

_____

_____

_____

_____

_____

How did you describe yourself? Was your description positive? Neutral? Or was it negative?

If you feel undeserving and have a poor opinion of yourself, it is now time to start building up your self-esteem.

Low self-esteem is having a negative viewpoint regarding oneself, and judging oneself to be unworthy. These deep-seated illogical beliefs will have a negative effect on every area of your life.

Once again your mind chatter will be feeding you negative and inappropriate thoughts about yourself. There may be deep-seated illogical beliefs which you think are true... but are not!

Recognising low self-esteem behaviours

Developing an awareness of low self-esteem behaviours enables you to begin to change.

No change is possible without first observing what we do, and how we act.

The following behaviours are evidence of room for improvement in our self-esteem.

- Taking offence easily
- Criticising or blaming others
- Talking negatively about self (beating yourself up)
- Experiencing excessive guilt
- Jealousy
- Not accepting compliments
- Failure to compliment others
- Putting ourselves last
- Failure to give or receive affection
- Comparing self to others
- Not asserting our feelings or rights when wronged
- Accepting verbal or physical abuse
- Constant poor health
- Dwelling on past failures
- Self-doubt

You must make a decision now to grow. Nothing changes without a **desire**, a **commitment** and then **action**! Be willing to confront what is stopping you, and overcome the negative self-talk.

Give yourself permission to fail sometimes. Perfection will always elude us... why? Because we are human and perfectly imperfect!

To appreciate your own worth is not egotism. A healthy, high self-esteem should not be confused with a big ego, which is more aligned with a swollen self-esteem, conceit and self-centredness.

The big ego is unhealthy, and is often low self-esteem in action. People with fragile, insecure esteems frequently overcompensate with a mask of confidence, self-possession and dominance. They may shout for attention, saying *"Hey, tell me how great I am... I've always been good at... I'm the best... You should do it my way"*. If people with big egos really believed all this, why do they feel the need to shout it out and to impress?

If their esteem were healthy they would already know they were good and wouldn't need to convince us – they would just 'be'. These people are very self-centred, and will only accommodate others' needs after their own are met. They must take care of number one first, because they lack the inner confidence and feelings of worth that permit a focus on others.

Healthy esteem

People with healthy esteem can focus on others' needs because they are comfortable and self confident. They will frequently appear selfless.

A healthy or high self-esteem is the basis of our ability to love others. It starts with self-acceptance, which is accepting that we are okay right now, with imperfections and blemishes, failures, regrets, dreams and desires. High self-esteem is knowing that we are good and it's okay to feel worthwhile. If someone else doesn't think so, it is their problem.

Self-respect is another element of self-esteem. It is the sum of our principles and values that guide our actions, and which build self-respect. When we act against these standards we are untrue to ourselves and act without integrity, and lose self-respect. When we violate our conscience we lower our feelings of self-esteem. The consequence is, we feel bad.

Comparing self to others to gain esteem is a shallow and useless strategy, as there will always be someone who has more of what you consider valuable. You are unique – one of a kind. There is no one like you.

There is a close relationship between self-esteem and success, high productivity, achievement, excellent performance or happiness. In other words, the healthier the self-esteem, the better we do! We attract to ourselves that which we feel worthy of receiving.

People with high self-esteem attract love, success and happiness. People with low self-esteem attract what they feel they deserve – other people with low self-esteem and poor treatment by others.

If you receive disrespect, ask yourself the question "Why have I allowed myself to be treated in this manner?"

DEVELOPING SELF-ESTEEM

If you want to improve your self-esteem, here are some steps to start empowering yourself:

- **Stop thinking negative thoughts about yourself**. Remember to rebut your inappropriate thoughts by writing in your journal. Also, write down three things about yourself that you are happy with.
- **Aim for accomplishments rather than perfection.** Give yourself a pat on the back for small accomplishments. Do something you are good at. No one is perfect. Each of us is unique. Appreciate yourself and be grateful for what you do have.
- **View mistakes as learning opportunities.** Accept that you will make mistakes because everyone does. Mistakes are part of learning. Remind yourself that a person's talents are constantly developing, and everyone excels at different things — it's what makes people interesting. Don't give up.
- **Try new things.** Get out of your comfort zone. Experiment with different activities that will help you get in touch with your talents. Then take pride in the new skills you develop.
- **Recognise what you can change and what you can't.** If you're unhappy with something about yourself that you can change, then start today. This might involve getting a new haircut, or new clothes. If it's something you can't change (like your height), then work towards loving yourself the way you are. All of us are perfectly imperfect.
- **Set goals.** Think about what you'd like to accomplish, then make a plan for how to do it. Stick with your plan and keep track of your progress. Make your goals SMART (specific,

measurable, attainable, realistic and time limited). For instance, say "I will lose 1kg per month for the next 3 months. By June 21st I will weigh......kg".

- **Take pride in your opinions and ideas.** Work on assertiveness. Ask for what you want.
- **Make a contribution.** Participate in an activity for a good cause, or volunteer your time in some other way. Join a group. Commit to a project. Take action. Feeling like you're making a difference and that your help is valued can do wonders to improve self-esteem.
- **Exercise!** You'll relieve stress, and be healthier and happier.
- **Have fun.** Enjoy spending time with the people you care about and doing the things you love. Relax and have a good time — and **stop holding yourself back.**

Also remember to use your affirmations, particularly "I like myself unconditionally".

Here are some other ways to build your self-esteem:

- Accept compliments.
- Give compliments and show appreciation, it costs you absolutely nothing.
- Give yourself a pat on the back, every day.
- Set your standards.
- Identify your values.
- Be your own first best friend (monitor your self-talk, identify your distorted ideas).
- Maintain your integrity – check on your ethics.
- Speak the truth. Let go of grudges and guilt.
- Forgive yourself as well as others (forgiveness is like a scalpel which removes emotional scars).
- Think about what you are good at. Focus on your good acts, your good deeds.

Personal self-esteem growth affirmations

Choose some of these affirmations, and say them aloud every day.

- I am worthy of love and happiness.
- I appreciate and love myself more every day.
- I always treat myself with respect.
- I am the most important person in my life.
- I have unlimited potential.
- I accept criticism well and forgive myself now.
- I am totally honest with myself and others.
- I am breaking free from the past.
- I accept my body as it is.
- I am open and caring towards others, and allow others to love and support me.
- I like myself unconditionally.

Write down some of your personal qualities. What are your strengths? How about your virtues?

_____

_____

_____

_____

Self-esteem plays a role in almost everything you do. People with high self-esteem do better in work and at school and find it easier to make friends. They tend to have better relationships. They feel happier and find it easier to deal with mistakes, disappointments and failures, and are more likely to stick with something until they succeed. The strategies listed above, when implemented, will make you feel better about yourself and help you make positive choices in your life

COMMUNICATION

Communication means 'to share'. Communication is the exchange and flow of information, feelings, ideas and thoughts between people.

Communication can be verbal or non-verbal. Non-verbal communication includes body language, hand gestures, eye movement, shaking of the head, nodding, smiling, and many other gestures or actions. Verbal communication is spoken communication as well as written words such as texting and email.

There are four things necessary for effective communication:

1. To be understood and to understand
2. To be respected and to respect
3. To be listened to and to listen
4. To be complete in the conversation (having said all you wanted to say)

It's crucial to learn to communicate exactly what it is you are feeling. This is greatly aided by having a confidant, a friend, or someone you can talk to openly and honestly. Recall the relief when you have something on your mind and you are able to talk about it. Self-disclosure – that is sharing your feelings, thoughts and problems with another will help you feel better. Joining a group is a great idea.

Undelivered communication is one of the biggest causes of upsets and stress. When we are in a state of depression we may fail to express our thoughts and feelings. If we have a low self-esteem, and feel helpless and powerless, our ability to share our feelings may be difficult. Let us look at ways to help you become more assertive, and express your feelings and thoughts.

Firstly, let us be clear on the difference between assertive and aggressive styles of communication.

Assertiveness

Assertiveness means communicating our ideas, thoughts and feelings in a confident, direct and honest way. It involves conveying our needs clearly without dominating, attacking or humiliating the other person. The other person's opinions will be listened to, without judgment, and good relationships become possible. An assertive person will look the other in the eye, maintaining an open, relaxed and attentive posture.

When we assert ourselves using clear messages, and are able to ask for what we need or want, we feel complete. When we set out to say something and we say it with courtesy and respect, and then it leads to us achieving a result or obtaining what we asked for, we feel satisfied.

If you fail to express yourself, or express yourself in a timid, apologetic way, the listener can easily disregard you, or even feel irritated with your submissive manner. You may not achieve your desired result, or have your needs or wants fulfilled. This may result in you feeling powerless, and even angry.

Practice looking at yourself in a mirror and asking politely for what you want – conveying your message without hesitancy, with a clear voice and while holding eye contact.

Aggressiveness

Aggressiveness refers to communicating in a dominating and demanding way which may violate the rights of others. The aggressor may humiliate, degrade or belittle others. They boost their own self-esteem and ego by putting others down. They may be rude, loud, abusive, and prefer attack to reasonable communication. Aggressive communication may involve finger pointing or stern expressions and can provoke feelings of hurt, embarrassment and humiliation in others.

How do you communicate?

_____
_____
_____
_____

'I' MESSAGES

When we need to confront a situation, there is an effective and non-attacking way called the 'I' message.

This typically begins by addressing the behaviour of the other, then a disclosure of our feelings, followed by a reason or an effect this behaviour has, and finally a request.

This is not a 'you' message, which immediately puts the other person on the defensive.

Rather, begin the sentence with 'When' or 'I feel' for instance:

"When you shout at me, I feel put down and humiliated, and the effect is that I am afraid to say anything. I'm asking that you stop shouting when communicating with me please."

This is not an attack on the person you are addressing. You didn't say *"You bully, shut up"* (which is probably what you were thinking). Of course, that is an attack, and not preferred at all.

Using the 'I' message approach you are simply conveying your feelings about the situation.

When.............. (say what behaviour caused the feeling)
I feel............ (insert a feeling word)
Because......... (describe the effect their behaviour is having)
Ideally, end this message with a
Request, or say 'I want', or 'I need' (what you want or need to happen)

Example: When trying to talk to your friend or parent, the other person tries to dominate and take over the conversation thereby limiting your participation in the discussion.

'You message' *(This is the one you are thinking)*
"*You are so full of yourself, I can't get a word in. For goodness sake shut up.*"

Behaviour	Feelings	Effects
Talking over me	frustrated	can't participate in discussion

'I' message:

"*When you talk over me, I feel frustrated because I can't say what I want to say. Can you please listen and let me give my viewpoint?*"

This type of confrontational message takes a little practice. The key is to remember to begin the sentence with '*When*' or even '*I feel*'. For example "*I feel disappointed when you leave your clothes all over the bedroom floor, because it makes our home untidy. Please will you pick them up?*"

You see, you did not attack them at all. You merely stated your feelings, and who can argue with your feelings? If you don't want to finish your sentence with "*I need or want*", you could ask, "*How can we work this out?*"

Write down some of your own 'I' messages. This will help you confront issues which you may have been avoiding.

When..
I feel..
Because..
I need, I would like, I want..

When...
I feel..
Because..
I need, I would like, I want..

When...
 feel..
Because..
I need, I would like, I want..

Remember to ask in a polite yet assertive manner.

The tongue Excerpt from *Sathya Sai Speak*, Sai Baba.

Of all the senses, the tongue has an overriding importance and influence. Mastery over this one sense organ will enable one to master easily all the other sense organs.

A horse can run fast, but once a bridle is put in its mouth and held tight, its entire movement can be easily controlled.

How is it that a small bridle is able to control such a large, strong and fast-running animal? Because the mouth is the most important and vulnerable part of the horse, from the standpoint of keeping it under control. Once the mouth is bridled, the entire animal comes under control. Likewise in a case of man also, the mouth is the most important among the five sense organs.

With the help of a small rudder, we can save a big boat from a fierce cyclone. The power of speech can be used either for a noble and sublime purpose, or misused in a mean and negative manner, that is for blessing or blaming others.

A "slip of the foot" may not cause much harm, but a "slip of the tongue'" may land you in hell!

A reckless use of your tongue can grievously hurt others' hearts for their entire life.

And no doctor on earth can heal the wound caused by a harsh word.

Always exercise control over your tongue, and never allow it to run amok. There is no need for verbal attacks, attack thoughts, or judgments. Attack thoughts generate depression.

INTEGRITY

Integrity is defined as the quality or state of being complete; in an unbroken condition; having wholeness, not corrupted. It is the quality or state of being unimpaired, in perfect condition, sound.

Take a bicycle wheel – when it has all its spokes, it is considered to have integrity. If we pull out two or three spokes, it loses its integrity. It no longer is whole.

For humans, having integrity is considered to include being of good character, and demonstrating characteristics such as sincerity, high moral principles, creativity, enthusiasm, tolerance, honesty and responsibility. People with integrity have strong ethics and values and happily contribute to the well being of others. They have a consistent commitment to doing the right thing. Integrity is also doing what you said you'd do, when you said you'd do it; that is, being reliable.

How do we lose this incredible state? Why do we let go of the very abilities that enable us to enjoy and win in life? We lose them by being unethical, by violating our integrity. We do this by not being true to our word, by not being reliable, by being dishonest, or taking what does not belong to us. In other words, through not being a 'good' person, and when this happens we become less 'whole'.

If we continue to be unethical, our abilities are lessened until we become a person who cannot create with power, who can no longer get enthused. Our tolerance becomes low, our ideas fixed, and we are unable to be energetic, happy or responsible. In short, one becomes a less powerful being who does not have the necessary abilities and qualities to handle life.

This personal diminishment is the effect of losing our integrity because our inner self is basically good, and observing or perceiving oneself to have caused harm, will, on an unconscious level, limit our abilities to prevent causing further harm.

Your integrity is the real you... mess around with it and violate it and you will end up feeling bad. By the same token, when you clean up your ethics and integrity you begin to feel good about yourself.

John, who was a character in a movie, gives us a perfect example of the way this works. John made a living as a money scammer. He took money illegally from any likely victim. Old, young, it did not matter. He chain smoked, and drank heavily every night. John had a number of health complaints. He developed stomach ulcers and had several psycho somatic problems too. This included compulsive obsessive door closing. He stuttered, had a problem with face tics (twitching and blinking), and he needed medication to go out and face the world. When John gave up stealing, and began working in a regular job, his health problems began to improve and he decided to quit smoking and drinking.

His conscience, or inner self was no longer violated. You see, when we do bad things, our conscience still operates. Our authentic self knows what is right and wrong. Fear, anxiety and guilt will take their toll on our body. Hence the word **dis-ease.** When we feel good about ourselves, there is nothing to fix, our health improves, and happiness ensues. Do what you feel is right, even if others are telling you it is not necessary, or that you are being taken advantage of. If you 'do the right thing' and feel clean about it, then you can take your attention off it to put on something else. **When we are ethical and have integrity, we experience no guilt and no fear.**

ATTACHMENT VERSUS COMMITMENT

Attachment

Attachment means 'fastened on' or 'fixed to' something else. When we are attached to an outcome, we are inflexible – we think 'this is it' and it's got to happen this particular way. We become fixed and positional. We cling to an addicted outcome. If our expectations are not met, we become anxious, angry, upset and dissatisfied.

Some side effects of being 'attached' are:

Anger
Confusion
Expectation
Disappointment
Dissatisfaction
Defensiveness
Driven,
Obsessiveness
A tendency to make people
right or wrong
Pain
Dogmatic opinions or behaviours
Low self-esteem

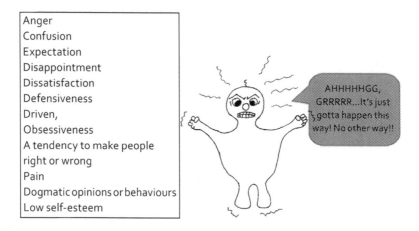

Commitment

Having commitment is to be involved in an obligation or pledge. It indicates a desire to do or perform. When commitment is present we have:

Love
Courage
Strength
Clarity
Selflessness
Listening
Freedom
Understanding
Integrity
Fun
Productivity
The ability to take 'no' for an answer
Persistence

Ok, so the plan has changed, no big deal, we can adapt ... It was just a plan anyhow!

When in 'breakdown' or if something stops you, just re-commit. **Don't be attached or addicted.** Getting upset is inappropriate, wasteful of energy and unproductive.

When we are committed to a result, and not attached, we no longer become emotionally upset. If something doesn't work out, try another way. It was just a plan that didn't work that time. When an expectation doesn't get fulfilled, ask yourself 'Am I attached to this?'.

**Stop the upset... just make a stand for commitment.
Relax... be yourself... stop trying so hard**

HISTORY

Another way of saying history is **his-story.** That is, the story of him, her, us. History is a record of events, a study of the past.

If you had a painful past and continue to relive the anguish today, this will keep you in a state of suffering and sadness. When we regurgitate and dwell on the past we are doing our creativity a disservice. If we are stuck in the past, how can we create in the present, in the now?

Being stuck in the past while trying to create the future is not compatible. If something happened to you, and you have not confronted it, or talked to someone, now is the time to do that. We must confront what disturbs us. Only when our issue is handled, and the emotional charge is released, can we move on.

It is only when we let go of the past and live in the present moment without attack thoughts that we can truly become happy. Don't allow your past to dictate your future. Your own mental health is at stake.

While remembering the past, think about **only the good things that happened to you, and the enjoyable events, and happy times.**

The present moment is always the only moment we have. When you align yourself with the present moment and let go of the past you are then free to be **anything or anyone you wish to be.**

When will you give up your 'story' about the past?

When will you break the chains of your emotional bondage?

This heavy load is preventing your happiness.

Get rid of it, get off it, get a new life... right now!

MOOD QUESTIONNAIRE

Please wait until you have completed at least four weeks of thought therapy, identifying and writing down your illogical thoughts, and doing the relaxation exercise every day before filling in this feeling questionnaire.

After four weeks, if you have done the homework every day, you will definitely show an improvement. Your depression will be improving moment by moment. You will feel lighter, happier and more motivated. Keep working. Persistence pays. Your recovery will happen.

Please read this booklet regularly. Each time you read it, you will gain even more insight.

I said that this course was simple, and it is. But I never said it was going to be easy.

It will take commitment and persistence, and then... the miracle will occur!

This does work. I used this method ten years ago, and continue to do so, to recover from my own depression, and have never relapsed since.

We invite you to once again record your score and notice what improvements have occurred during this course.

Keeping score of how you feel out of ten

Name

Date

Mood

I feel sad and gloomy 1 2 3 4 5 6 7 8 9 10 I'm the happiest I've ever felt

Confidence

I feel like hiding in a corner 1 2 3 4 5 6 7 8 9 10 I could stand up and give a public speech

Self esteem

I feel worthless 1 2 3 4 5 6 7 8 9 10 I'm on top of the world

How much I feel like changing

I can't be bothered to do anything 1 2 3 4 5 6 7 8 9 10 I want a big life makeover

Hope for the future

I can't believe anything will get better 1 2 3 4 5 6 7 8 9 10 I'm very hopeful life will be better

Add up the numbers, record your score.............................

Do not judge

Did you attain a higher score than at the start? I hope so.

Continue to apply the methods given in this book, and know that you cannot afford the luxury of a negative thought. Ask yourself "Is this an attack thought?". If it is, then get off it!

Become alert – aware of your thoughts, as well as your emotions.

To sustain real and lasting change we must change our thoughts, feelings and behaviour.

Mastery of your mind takes practice, practice, practice... that's all.

IN A NUTSHELL

- Go about your life peacefully, even though there may be emotional people around you.
- Avoid aggressive people, they will upset your peace of mind.
- Stay true to yourself, be honest and ethical. You will feel better about yourself.
- Treat others with respect and listen attentively to their communication, even though it sometimes may not interest you.
- Speak clearly with courtesy, manners and respect, say what you want to say, ask for what you want.
- Nail those wrong and toxic thoughts. Don't accept that what your mind is saying is true. This is strange but the actual truth.
- Get out of your comfort zone, do something different right now.
- You are perfectly imperfect... do not compare yourself with others. There will always be someone else with more of what you consider valuable. Learn to love yourself, with all your imperfections.
- Stay in control of your thinking, and stop imagining negative events. Your thoughts will create your reality. Why would you want a miserable life?
- Stay at peace, relax and meditate regularly. Your body heals itself when it is completely quiet and relaxed.
- Do not dwell on the past, think only of the good things you did and the good things that were done to you. Give up the rest.

You deserve peace, fun, joy and prosperity. Ask for it, deserve it, and receive it!

Don't seek happiness. If you seek it, you won't find it. Happiness is elusive, but freedom from unhappiness is attainable now.

Unhappiness covers up your natural and authentic self of well being and inner peace, the source of true happiness.

What we vividly imagine, truly desire, declare, and consistently take actions on will inevitably happen.

Keep at it... this does work!
No attack thoughts towards yourself or others
No physical attack and no verbal attack
Practice being non-reactive
Forgive

If you are depressed, you are living in the past.
If you are anxious, you are living in the future.
If you are at peace, you are living in the present.

Lao Tzu

REFERENCES

Adair, M. (1984) Working Inside Out, Tools for Change. California, Wingbow Press

Atkinson, S. (2005) Climbing out of Depression. Lion Hudson, Oxford, England.

Australian College of Applied Psychology, Sydney, Australia. Mood Questionnaire

Beck, A.T. (1976) Cognitive therapies and emotional disorders. New York: New American Library.

British Association for Behavioural and Cognitive Psychotherapies (BABCP) Mapping Psyhotherapy. (2005). What is CBT. Found online at http://www.babcp.com/silo/files/what-is-cbt-.pdf

Brown, J.D. (1993) Self Esteem, The Puzzle of Low Self Regard, New York, Plenum Press

Bradshaw, J. (1992) Self-love. New York: Bantam Books

Burns, D. D. (1980) Feeling good: The new mood therapy. New York: New American Library.

Burns, D.D., M.D. (1990, 1999) The Feeling Good Handbook. Plume, USA

Cormac Series Published by Cormac Publications, PO box 651 Burleigh Heads, QLD 4220. 1970

Illustrations & text Copyright Cormac Publications.

All rights reserved ISBN 0 949261 02 5 Printed and typeset by: Jon The Printer, 7 United Road, Ashmore, Qld 4215

De Vito, J.A. (1998) The interpersonal Communication Book (9th ed) New York: Longman

Grant, A.M. & Green, J. (2001) It's your life. What are you going to do with it? Biddles Ltd. Guildford. U.K.

Hambly, Dr.K. (2001) How to improve your Confidence, London, Sheldon Press

Hardin, K. & Hall, M. (2011) Queer Blues, The Lesbian & Gay guide to overcoming depression. Oakland California, New Harbinger Publications Inc.

Hermes, S. (M.Ed. L.A.C.)(1997) Assertiveness Workbook, Practical skills for positive communication. Hazelden Publishing, Centre City, Minnesota, USA.

Johnstone, M. (2012) Quiet the Mind, an Illustrated guide on How to Meditate, Sydney, Pan Macmillan Aust. Pty. Ltd

Sathya Sai, S. (1969) Sathya Sai Speaks: Discourses by Sri Sathya Sai Baba, Sri Sathya Sai Books and Publications Trust, Prashanti Nilayam, India.

Tolle, E. (2005) A New Earth, Awakening to your Life's purpose, Australia, Penguin Group

Wimbush, K. (1994) The Wimbush Files. Comfort Zones, Ethics and Integrity. Wimbush & Associates, San Jose, California.

ABOUT THE AUTHOR

Jan Hayes is a creative designer and painter. She formerly owned and ran an executive business and life coaching company in Sydney, Australia. She now lives in Mandurah, Western Australia and enjoys sailing, travelling and renovating houses.

Jan is happily married to Neil, who is her best mate, devoted husband and biggest supporter. She has a son and extended family in Australia and overseas.

Following her own experience with recurring bouts of depression, Jan was inspired to write an interactive self-help workbook to help other people overcome this common affliction. She has long been curious about human behaviour, and for many years studied Psychology and Sociology. Through combining some well-known methods with several of her own techniques in this practical workbook, Jan has created a fresh and unique approach to bring about recovery from depression. She has also conducted a number of workshops about the methods described here.

Jan's illustrations also feature in this booklet.

Jan hopes those suffering with depression find these techniques as useful as she did.

"Within weeks of beginning my program of self observation, identifying thoughts and changing my thinking, I began a new way of living, and immediately felt better."

Jan's depression has never returned. She does not expect it to.